Floating Point Computation

Patrick H. Stakem

© 2013

3rd edition

4th in Computer Architecture Series

Table ofContents

Introduction

This book discusses the floating point data format in computation. It is somewhat architecture-neutral, but does restrict the discussion to binary computation in digital computers based on software and microelectronics technology. To understand why we need the complexity of floating point for scientific, engineering, and financial calculations, we need to review number systems, integer calculations in binary and decimal, and other representations systems, as well as the concept of negative numbers and zero. This work contains a broad but not comprehensive list of floating point units and software packages.

Now-a-days, it is normal to find a floating point unit as default. The next step is the graphics processing chips, sometimes called AI chips, used for image processing. Odds are, you have has one on your phone

The author

The author received his BSEE from Carnegie Mellon University, and Masters in Computer Science and Applied Physics from the Johns Hopkins University. He has always worked in the aerospace sector, supporting NASA projects at all of the NASA Centers. He has taught for the graduate Engineering Science and Computer Science Departments at Loyola University in Maryland, and Embedded Systems for the Johns Hopkins

University, Whiting School of Engineering, Engineering for Professionals Program.

He was introduced to the problems of floating point computation in his work for the Department of Applied Space Science at Carnegie, where certain dynamics calculations for the IMP-I spacecraft required more than double precision. He implemented a quadruple-precision floating point package for a large mainframe system.

The author is an engineer, not a mathematician. He uses math as a tool, not as an enjoyment. This book is dedicated to his friend, colleague, and boss, William Kelly. He taught me the difference between a mathematician and an engineer, and the important difference between a developer and a tester. Bill helped develop the NASA tracking ships for the manned missions, before NASA had tracking satellites. He really would have enjoyed criticizing this book. Unfortunately, he passed away from brain cancer, while applying NASA-developed image enhancement techniques to medical imaging, which could have saved him.

Also, thanks are due to the many students who took my courses in Computer Architecture and Engineering, and who helped find errors and omissions in the material.

Mr. Stakem can be found on Facebook and Linkedin.

Photo credits

The equation on the front cover comes from Quantum Electrodynamics, and describes a spin ½ field interacting with a Electromagnetic field.

Although we might be fairly adept at manipulating numbers, we need to understand how machinery, most importantly electronic computers, represent and manipulate numbers. You can skip over these sections if you know this already.

Number representation in computing machinery

A *bit* is the smallest unit of binary information. It represents a yes/no, on/off, left/right, north/south type of decision. It can be represented in mathematics as the digits zero or one. Any technology that can represent two states can represent a bit. Red light/green light, voltage or no voltage, current or no current, light or darkness, north magnetic or south magnetic, etc. We have to be careful to distinguish between the mathematical concept of a bit (one of two possible states) and its implementation.

Also, we don't necessarily need to use base-2 for computers, but it matches the implementation in microelectronics fairly well. Early computers (and calculators) used base-10, which we use because we have ten fingers.

Charles Babbage's mechanical computers of the mid 19th century used decimal notation. The binary system was known, but Boole and DeMorgan hadn't worked out all the details in using logic for calculation, and there was the conversion issue. At the cost of complexity, just build the machinery in decimal. Babbage's major project, the

Analytical Engine, has yet to be built, but there is an active project to get it done by the 150th anniversary of his death. The project is called Plan 28.

The choice of a base number in mathematics will influence how easy or hard it is to manipulate the numbers. If we just want to know that we have 1 sheep, 2 sheep, or many sheep, we don't need very sophisticated math. The ancient Babylonians used a base-60 math, which survives in the way we tell time (seconds, minutes). They also had computers, abacus units designed to handle their representation. The Romans did not use a positional number system, which is why it is very hard to do long division in Roman numerals.

A *positional number system* allows us to choose a base number, and use the number digits to represent different orders of magnitude, even fractions. In Roman numerals, we have a specific symbol for fifty, and that is "L". In decimal, we use "50." That is to say, 5 x 10 (the base) plus 0 times 1.

We also need to consider the important concept of zero, which was used in Mesoamerica, China, India, and other places. The Romans had the concept of zero, just not a specific symbol for it. The zero symbol become important in positional notation, to keep the symbols in the right place, not just to indicate that we have no sheep.

We like to use ten as a base, because we have ten fingers. Actually, we can use any number for a base. The ones of interest to use in computing are base-2 and base-16. For microelectronics, the base-2 is used, because the physics of the devices allow for representation and recognition of two different states easily and efficiently. Base-16 is for our convenience (keep telling yourself that.)

So we like to use base 10 and computers like to use base 2, we need to discuss how to convert numbers between these bases.

Bytes, Words, and other collections

A *byte* is a collection of 8 bits. This makes for a handy size. In binary, a byte can represent 1 of 256 (2^8) possible states or values.

A computer *word* is a collection of 8, 16, 24, 13, 97, or some other number of bits. The number of bits collected into a word does not need to be a power of two. The range of numbers we can represent depends on how many bits we have in the word. This determines the complexity of the implementation.

Integers

All the numbers we talk about will be *integers* (until we get to floating point). Integers have a finite range. Eight bits gives us 256 (2^8) numbers, and 16 bits gives us nearly 65000. We need to give up one bit (or, 1/2 our range of numbers) for a sign position. There will more discussion of this in the floating point section.

One thing to keep in mind is that the hardware keeps track of the bookkeeping for integer mathematical operations. The binary point is assumed to be on the right side of the word. This means there are no fractional parts. We can, in software, choose to have the binary point anywhere in the word, in which case the bookkeeping problem is ours, in the software. For example, for addition or subtraction, the binary points of the two values must be aligned. This technique is referred to as *scaled integer* representation. The programmer always has to keep in mind what the hardware does to the integers.

Another technique is used to simplify the processing of angles. Recall that our angles are decimal, but we use 360 degrees, or 2 X Pi radians. In binary, we can use binary radians, where we divide the circle into 256 or 1024. Calculations can be done on these *binary radian* ("brad") values quickly and efficiently, and the final conversion to decimal degrees or angles done at the end of the calculation, if required.

BCD Format

Binary Coded Decimal uses 10 of the possible 16 codes in 4 bits. The other bit patterns are not used, or could be used to indicate sign, error, overflow, or such. BCD converts to decimal easily, and provides a precise representation of decimal numbers. It requires serial by digit calculations, but gives exact results. It uses more storage than binary integers, and the implementation of the logic for operations is a bit more complex. It is an alternative to the limited range or precision of binary integers, and the complexity of floating point. BCD is used extensively in instrumentation and personal calculators. Support for operations on BCD numbers was provided in IBM mainframes, and the Intel x86 ISA.

BCD 4 bit code, 10 valid values:

$0000 = 0$, $0001 = 1$, $0010 = 2$, $0011 = 3$, $0100 = 4$
$0101 = 5$, $0110 = 6$, $0111 = 7$, $1000 = 8$, $1001 = 9$

1010, 1011, 1100, 1101, 1110, 1111 = invalid number codes

BCD numbers (4 bits) can be stored in a byte, which uses more storage, but makes calculations easier. These are sometimes referred to as BCD nibbles. Alternately, BCD digits can be packed 2 to a byte.

Arithmetic operations in BCD format numbers are usually done in binary, and then adjusted to handle the carry (or borrow). For example, in packed BCD, we may generate a carry between the 3rd and 4th bit position. Subtraction is usually implemented by adding the 10's complement of the subtrahend. The 10's complement is formed by taking the 9's complement, and then adding one. The 9's complement can be formed by subtracting the digits from 9. If a BCD arithmetic operation generates an invalid BCD result, the number 6 can be added to force a carry. BCD strings of numbers can have a "decimal point" inserted wherever convenient. Additional bookkeeping is then needed to keep the numbers commensurate for addition and subtraction, and to adjust in multiplication and division.

Prefixes

There are standard metric system (SI) prefixes used to represent orders of magnitude in decimal. The same prefixes are used to designate binary powers, but are not part of the SI system.

The prefixes are defined for decimal values, but are also applied to binary numbers. The percent difference is not much, but in the larger magnitudes, can be significant. When someone in the computer or communications industry quotes you a number of giga-something, stop them and ask if that is decimal or binary.

Generally, memory size is measured in the powers of two, and communication speed measured in decimal powers. Hard disk sizes are specified in decimal units. Computer clock frequencies are usually specified in decimal.

Prefix	Decimal	Binary	deviation
K = kilo	10^3	2^{10}	2.4%
M = mega	10^6	2^{20}	4.9%
G = giga	10^9	2^{30}	7.4%
T = tera	10^{12}	2^{40}	10%
P = peta	10^{15}	2^{50}	12.6%

E = exa 10^{18} 2^{60} *15.3%*

To date, there has been no reported major failure related to misinterpreting or confusion over prefix units. There have been class action lawsuits regarding confusing information on packaging.

Positional notation

In a *positional number system*, the same symbols are used in different positions to represent multiples of the powers of the base. It is a system for representing numbers by symbols. An alternative, such as Roman numerals, is not a positional system, with unique symbols for different values. Our Arabic-derived decimal number system is positional. The Babylonians used a positional number system with base 60. The Maya used base 20.

A number system of a certain base, N, needs N symbols. At the right hand side of our decimal numbers, we have a *decimal point*. This separates the positive from the negative powers of the base (i.e., fractions). Similarly, we can have an *octal point* or a *hexadecimal point* or a *binary point*. By convention, digits to the left represent high values of the base.

The decimal systems uses ten unique symbols to represent quantities (0,1,2,3,4,5,6,7,8,9). The binary system uses two (0,1).

13

Overflow

Overflow is the case where a calculation has produced a result that is larger in magnitude than can be held in a finite register or storage location. It is a result of using a finite number system, such as 16-bits. Adding two of the largest numbers in 16-bits will result in a 17-bit number, for example. A carry is a type of overflow indicator.

Underflow is a condition where the result is smaller in value than the smallest representable number. This can't happen in binary, but can occur in floating point representation.

Infinities, overflows, and underflows

Infinity is the largest number that can be represented in the number system. Adding 1 to infinity results in infinity, by definition. In a closed number system imposed by the finite word size of the computer, adding one to infinity results in an *overflow*, a change of sign.

Negative infinity is the most negative number that can be represented in the number system, not the smallest number.

The least positive number, or the smallest amount that can be represented in the finite number systems is 1. That is because the numbers are usually considered integers, with the binary point on the right of the word. In floating point representation it is different; this will be discussed in the floating point section.

Overflow is the condition in a finite word size machine, where the result of an arithmetic operation is too large to fit in the register. For example, when adding two of the largest positive numbers in a 16-bit representation, the result would not fit in 16 bits. With the use of a two's complement representation scheme for negative numbers, the overflow would result in a sign change, from a large positive to a small negative number.

Underflow is a condition where, as the result of an arithmetic operation, the result is smaller in value than the smallest representable number. The result will be reported as zero in integer representation, even if it is positive, greater than zero, but less than 1. The resolution of binary integers is 1.

Elementary Math operations

The elementary mathematical operations include add, subtract, multiply, and divide.

<u>The laws of binary addition</u>

0+0=0
1+0=1
0+1=1
1+1=0 (with a carry)

Laws of binary subtraction (Remember a-b does not equal b-a)

0-0=0
0-1=1 (with a borrow)
1-0=1
1-1=0

Laws of binary multiplication

0 x 0 = 0
0 x 1 = 0
1 x 0 = 0
1 x 1 = 1

(that's easy; anything times 0 is 0))

Laws of binary division

(Division by zero is not defined. There is no answer.)

0 / 0 = not allowed
1 / 0 = not allowed
0 / 1 = 0
1 / 1 = 1

Floating point

This section describes the *floating point* number representation, and explains when it is used, and why. Floating point is an old computer technique for gaining dynamic range in scientific and engineering calculations, at the cost of accuracy. First, we look at fixed point, or integer, calculations to see where the limitations are. Then, we'll examine how floating point helps expand the limits.

In a finite word length machine, there is a tradeoff between dynamic range and accuracy in representation. The value of the most significant bit sets the dynamic range because the effective value of the most positive number is infinity. The value of the least significant bit sets the accuracy, because a value less than the LSB is zero. And, the MSB and the LSB are related by the word length.

In any fixed point machine, the number system is of a finite size. For example, in 18 bit word, we can represent the positive integers from 0 to $2^{18}-1$, or 262,143. A word of all zeros = 0, and a word of all ones = 262,143. I'm using 18 bits as an example because it's not too common. There's nothing magic about 8, 16, or 32 bit word sizes.

If we want to use signed numbers, we must give up one bit to represent the sign. Of course, giving up one bit halves the number of values available in the representation. For a signed integer in an 18 bit word, we can represent integers from + to - 131,072. Of course, zero is also a valid number. Either the positive range or the negative range must give up a digit so we can represent zero. For now, let's say that in 18 bits, we can represent the integers from -131,072 to 131,071.

There are several ways of using the sign bit for representation. We can have a sign-magnitude format, a

1's complement, or a 2's complement representation. Most computers use the 2's complement representation. This is easy to implement in hardware. In this format, to form the negative of a number, complement all of the bits (1->0, 0->1), and add 1 to the least significant bit position. This is equivalent to forming the 1's complement, and then adding one. One's complement format has the problem that there are two representations of zero, all bits 0 and all bits 1. The hardware has to know that these are equivalent. This added complexity has led to 1's complement schemes falling out of use in favor of 2's complement. In two's complement, there is one representation of zero (all bits zero), and one less positive number, than the negatives. (Actually, since zero is considered positive, there are the same number. But, the negative numbers have more range.) This is easily illustrated for 3 bit numbers, and can be extrapolated to any other fixed length representation.

Remember that the difference between a signed and an unsigned number lies in our interpretation of the bit pattern.

Interpretation of 4-bit patterns

Up to this point we have considered the bit patterns to represent integer values, but we can also insert an arbitrary binary point (analogous to the decimal point) in the word. For integer representations, we have assumed the binary point to lie at the right side of the word, below the LSB. This gives the LSB a weight of 2^0, or 1, and the msb has a weight of 2^{16}. (The sign bit is in the 2^{17}

position). Similarly, we can use a fractional representation where the binary point is assumed to lie between the sign bit and the MSB, the MSB has a weight of 2^{-1}, and the LSB has a weight of 2^{-17}.

The MSB sets the range, the LSB sets the accuracy, and the LSB and MSB are related by the word length. For cases between these extremes, the binary point can lie anywhere in the word, or for that matter, outside the word. For example, if the binary point is assumed to be 2 bits to the right of the LSB, the LSB weight, and thus the precision, is 2^2. The MSB is then 2^{19}. We have gained dynamic range at the cost of precision. If we assume the binary point is to the left of the MSB, we must be careful to ignore the sign, which does not have an associated digit weight. For an assumed binary point 2 bit positions to the right of the MSB, we have a MSB weight of 2^{-3}, and an LSB weight of 2^{-20}. We have gained precision at the cost of dynamic range.

It is important to remember that the computer does not care where we assume the binary point to be. It simply treats the numbers as integers during calculations. We overlay the bit weights and the meanings.

A 16-bit integer can represent the values between -16384 to 16383

A 32-bit integer can represent the values between $-2*10^9$ to $2*10^9$

A short real number has the range 10^{-37} to 10^{38} in 32 bits.

A long real number has the range 10^{-307} to 10^{308} in 64 bits

19

We can pack 18 decimal (BCD) digits, with sign, into 80 bits.

To add or subtract scaled values, they must have the same scaling factor; they must be commensurate. If the larger number is normalized, the smaller number must be shifted to align it for the operation. This may have the net result of adding or subtracting zero, as bits fall out the right side of the small word. This is like saying that 10 billion + .00001 is approximately 10 billion, to 13 decimal places of accuracy.

In multiplication, the scaling factor of the result is the sum of the scaling factors of the products. This is analogous to engineering notation, where we learn to add the powers of 10.

In division, the scaling factor of the result is the difference between the scaling factor of the dividend and the scaling factor of the divisor. The scaling factor of the remainder is that of the dividend. In engineering notation, we subtract the powers of 10 for a division.

In a normal form for a signed integer, the most significant bit is one. This says, in essence, that all leading zeros have been squeezed out of the number. The sign bit does not take part in this procedure. However, note that if we know that the most significant bit is always a one, there is no reason to store it. This gives us a free bit in a sense; the most significant bit is a 1 by definition, and the msb-1 th bit is adjacent to the sign bit. This simple trick has doubled the effective accuracy of the word, because each bit position is a factor of two.

The primary operation that will cause a loss of precision or accuracy is the subtraction of two numbers that have nearly but not quite identical values. This is commonly encountered in digital filters, for example, where successive readings are differenced. For an 18 bit word, if the readings differ in, say, the 19th bit position, then the difference will be seen to be zero. On the other hand, the scaling factor of the parameters must allow sufficient range to hold the largest number expected. Care must be taken in subtracting values known to be nearly identical. Precision can be retained by pre-normalization of the arguments.

During an arithmetic operation, if the result is a value larger than the greatest positive value for a particular format, or less than the most negative, then the operation has overflowed the format. Normally, the absolute value function cannot overflow, with the exception of the absolute value of the least negative number, which has no corresponding positive representation, because we made room for the representation of zero.

In addition, the scaling factor can increase by one, if we consider the possibility of adding two of the largest possible numbers. We can also consider subtracting the largest (absolute value) negative number from the largest (in an absolute sense) negative number.

A one bit position left shift is equivalent to multiplying by two. Thus, after a one position shift, the scaling factor must be adjusted to reflect the new position of the binary point. Similarly, a one bit position right shift is equivalent to division by two, and the scaling factor must be similarly adjusted after the operation.

Numeric overflow occurs when a non-zero result of an arithmetic operation is too small in absolute value to be represented. The result is usually reported as zero. The subtraction case discussed above is one example. Taking the reciprocal of the largest positive number is another.

As in the decimal representation, some numbers cannot be represented exactly in binary, regardless of the precision. Non-terminating fractions such as 1/3 are one case, and the irrational numbers such as e and pi are another. Operations involving these will result in inexact results, regardless of the format. However, this is not necessarily an error. The irrationals, by definition, cannot exactly be represented by a ratio of integers. Even in base 10 notation, e and pi extend indefinitely.

When the results of a calculation do not fit within the format, we must throw something away. We normally delete bits from the right (or low side) side of the word (the precision end). There are several ways to do this. If we simply ignore the bits that won't fit within the format, we are *truncating*, or rounding toward zero. We choose the closest word within the format to represent the results. We can also round up by adding 1 to the LSB of the resultant word if the first bit we're going to throw away is a 1. We can also choose to round to even, round to odd, round to nearest, round towards zero, round towards + infinity, or round towards - infinity. Consistency is the desired feature. Rounding modes can include round to nearest, round to minus infinity, round to plus infinity, round to zero, round to nearest, and round away from zero.

Rounding error can have costly and fatal consequences, A terrible incident in the Patriot Missile System in the first Gulf War was due to accumulated mathematical error. A Patriot anti-missile failed to intercept an incoming missile, and 28 American troops died. This was due to clock drift, as the missile battery had been active for over 100 hours, and the clock was off by a little more than .3 seconds, or about 0.5 kilometers for the position of the incoming missile. The clock time was kept in integer format, and converted to floating point, with accumulated error.

In another high-profile error, the launch of the first Ariane-V rocket ended some 30 seconds into the mission, resulting in a loss of the vehicle and payloads, worth about $500 million. The cause was traced to a unit that failed, and sent a diagnostic code to the main controller. The diagnostic code was incorrectly converted into floating point format, and caused the vehicle's steering motors to go hard over to one side.

If we look at typical physical constants, we can get some idea of the dynamic range that we'll require for typical applications. The mass of an electron, you recall, is 9.1085×10^{-31} grams. Avogadro's number is 6.023×10^{23}. If we want to multiply these quantities, we need a dynamic range of $10^{(23+31)} = 10^{54}$, which would require a 180 bit word (10^{54} approx.$= 2^{180}$). Most of the bits in this 180 bit word would be zeros as place holders. Well, since zeros don't mean anything, can't we get rid of them? Of course.

We need dynamic range, and we need precision, but we usually don't need them simultaneously. The floating point data structure will give us dynamic range, at the cost of being unable to exactly represent data.

So, finally, we talk about floating point. In essence, we need a format for the computer to work with that is analogous to engineering notation, a mantissa and a power of ten. The two parts of the word, with their associated signs, will take part in calculation exactly like the scaled integers discussed previously. The exponent is the scaling factor that we used. Whereas in scaled integers, we had a fixed scaling factor, in floating point, we allow the scaling factor to be carried along with the word, and to change as the calculations proceed.

The representation of a number in floating point, like the representation in scientific notation, is not unique. For example,

$$6.54 \times 10^2 = .654 \times 10^3 = 654. \times 10^0$$

We have to choose a scheme and then be consistent. What is normally done is that the exponent is defined to be a number such that the leftmost digit in the mantissa is non-zero. This is defined as the normal form.

In the floating point representation, the number of bits assigned to the exponent determines *dynamic range*, and the number of bits assigned to the mantissa determine the *precision*, or resolution. For a fixed word size, we must allocate the available bits between the precision (mantissa), and the range (exponent).

Granularity is defined as the difference between representable numbers. This term is normally equal to the absolute precision, and relates to the least significant bit.

Denormalized numbers

This topic is getting well into number theory, and I will only touch on these special topics here. There is a use for numbers that are not in normal form, so-called denormals. This has to do with decreasing granularity. A *denorm* has an exponent which is the smallest representable exponent, with a leading digit of the mantissa not equal to zero. An un-normalized number, on the other hand, has the same mantissa, but an exponent which is not the smallest representable. Let's get back to engineering...

Overflow and Underflow

If the result of an operation results in a number too large (in an absolute magnitude case) to be represented, we have generated an overflow. If the result is too small to be represented, we have an underflow. Results of an overflow can be reported as infinity (+ or - as required), or as an error bit pattern. The underflow case is where we have generated a denormalized number. The IEEE standard, discussed below, handles denorms as valid operands. Another approach is to specify resultant denorms as zero.

<u>Standards</u>

There are many standards for the floating point representation, with the IEEE standard being the defacto industry choice. In this section, we'll discuss the IEEE standard in detail, and see how some other industry standards differ, and how conversions can be made.

IEEE floating point

The IEEE standard specifies the representation of a number as +/- mantissa x $2^{(+/- \text{ exponent})}$. Note that there are two sign bits, one for the mantissa, and one for the exponent. Note also that the exponent is an exponent of two, not ten. This is referred to as radix-2 representation. Other radices are possible. The most significant bit of the mantissa is assumed to be a 1, and is not stored. Take a look at what this representation buys us. A 16 bit integer can cover a range of +/- 10^4. A 32 bit integer can span a range of +/- 10^9. The IEEE short real format, in 32 bits, can cover a range of +/- $10^{+/-38}$. A 64 bit integer covers the range +/- 10^{19}. A long real IEEE floating point number covers the range +/- $10^{+/- 308}$. The dynamic range of calculations has been vastly increased for the same data size. What we have lost is the ability to exactly represent numbers, but we are close enough for engineering.

In the short, real format, the 32 bit word is broken up into fields. The mantissa, defined as a number less than 1, occupies 23 bits. The most significant bit of the data item is the sign of the mantissa. The exponent occupies 8 bits. The represented word is as follows:

$$(-1)^S \ (2^{E+bias}) \ (F1...F23)$$

where F0...F23 < 1. Note that F0=1 by definition, and is not stored.

The term $(-1)^S$ gives us + when the S bit is 0 and - when the S bit is 1. The bias term is defined as 127. This is used instead of a sign bit for the exponent, and achieves the same results. This format simplifies the hardware, because only positive numbers are then involved in exponent calculations. As a side benefit, this approach ensures that reciprocals of all representable numbers can be represented.

In the long real format, the structure is as follows:

$$(-1)^S \ (2^{E+bias}) \ (F1...F52)$$

where F0...F52 < 1. Note that F0=1 by definition, and is not stored.

Here, the bias term is defined as 1023.

For intermediate steps in a calculation, there is a temporary real data format in 80 bits. This expands the exponent to 15 bits, and the mantissa to 64 bits. This allows a range of +/- 10^{4932}, which is a large number in anyone's view.

In the IEEE format, provision is made for entities known as *Not-A-Number* (NaN's). For sample, the result of trying to multiply zero times infinity is NaN. These entities are status signals that particular violation cases took place. IEEE representation also supports four user select-able rounding modes. What do we do with results that won't fit in the bits allocated? Do we round or truncate? If we round, is it towards +/- infinity, or zero? Not all implementations of the IEEE standard implement all of the modes and options.

Floating point hardware is specialized, optimized computer architecture for the floating point data structure. It usually features concurrent operation with host, or the integer unit. Initially, floating point units were separate chips, but now the state of the art allows these functional units to be included on the same silicon real estate as the integer processor. The hardware of the floating point unit is specialized to handle the floating point data format. For example, in a floating multiply, we simultaneously integer multiply the mantissas and add the exponents. A barrel shifter is handy for normalization /renormalization by providing a shift of any number of bits in one clock period. Floating point units usually implement the format conversions in hardware (integer to floating, Float; floating to integer, Fix), and can handle extended precision (64 bit) integers. Both external and internal floating point units usually rely on the main processor's instruction fetch unit. The coprocessor may have to do a memory access for load/store. In this case, it may use a dma-like protocol to get use of the memory bus resource from the integer processor.

Floating point hardware gives us the ability to add, subtract, multiply, and sometimes divide. Some units provide only the reciprocal function, which is a simple divide into a known fixed quantity (1), and thus easy to implement. A divide requires two operations, then, a reciprocal followed by a multiply. Some units also include square root, and some transcendental primitives. In general, these functions are implemented in a microstep fashion, with Taylor or other series expansions of the functions of interest.

signed integer range - $2^{(\text{number of bits - 1})}$

10 bits - 1 x 10^3 (a good approximation is 2^{10} is approximately 10^3)

16 bits - 3 x 10^4

32 bits - 2 x 10^9

64 bits - 9.2 x 10^{18}

128 bits - 1.7 x 10^{38}

256 bits - 1.1 x 10^{77}

Floating Point operations

This subsection discuses operations on floating point numbers. This forms the basis for the specification of a floating point emulation software package, or for the development of custom hardware.

Before the addition can be performed, the floating point numbers must be *commensurate* with addition; in essence, they must have the same exponent. The mantissa of the number with the smaller exponent will be right shifted, and the exponent adjusted accordingly. However, if the right shift is equal to or more than the number of bits in the mantissa representation, we will lose something. This is analogous to the case where we add 0.000001 to 1 million and get approximately 1 million.

After the addition of mantissas, we may need to right shift the resultant by 1, and adjust the exponent accordingly, to account for mantissa overflow. This is analogous to the case of adding $4.1 \times 10^{16} + 6.3 \times 10^{16}$, with the result of 10.4×10^{16}, or 1.04×10^{17}, in normal form.

If we add two numbers of almost equal magnitude but opposite sign, we get a case of massive cancellation. Here, the leading digits of the mantissa may be zero, with a loss of precision. Renormalization is always called for after addition.

example: $1.23456 * 10^{16}$ plus $-1.23455 * 10^{16} = 0.00001 \times 10^{16}$, or $1.0 * 10^{11}$, in normal form.

In multiply, we may simultaneously multiply the mantissas, and add the exponents. After the operation, we need to renormalize the results. In division, we divide the mantissas and subtract the exponents, then renormalize.

The easiest division to do is a *reciprocal*, where the dividend is a known quantity, 1. Some systems implement only the reciprocal operation, requiring a following multiplication to complete the division operation. Even so, this may be faster than a division, because the reciprocal is much easier to implement in algorithmic form than the general purpose division.

Transcendentals

The floating point unit can also implement *transcendental functions*. These are usually represented as Taylor series expansions of common trigonometric and log functions. Enough transcendentals are included to provide basis functions for all we might need to calculate.

- F2XM1 = 2^{X-1}
- FYL2X = Y * $\log_2$ (X)
- FYL2XP1 = Y * $\log_2$ (X+1)
- FPTAN = tangent
- FPATAN = arctangent

From the basis functions, if x=tan(a), then a = atan (x), and

- Sin (a) = x / sqrt (1 + x^2)
- Cos (a) = 1 / sqrt (1 + x^2)
- Asin (x) = atan [x / sqrt (1-x^2)]

There are known functions to calculate 2^x, e^x, 10^x, and y^x in terms of the F2MX1 (2^x-1) function. Similarly, the log base e and base 10 can be calculated in terms of the FYL2X (log base 2) function. All of the trigonometric, inverse trigonometric, hyperbolic, and inverse hyperbolic functions can be calculated in terms of the supplied basis functions.

Formats

In the beginning, each computer manufacturer such as IBM, Univac, and DEC defined their own floating point format, and these were generally incompatible with those of other manufacturers. Add to this the confusion caused by varying word sizes, such as 6- versus 8-bits. Conversion between formats was a complicated process. The earliest microprocessors, 8-bit machines, did not support floating point format, but could do 8-bit arithmetic, and BCD. Floating point was provided by software libraries, such as one for the Intel 8080 machine, from Lawrence Livermore Labs. Doing the calculations in software was a slow process, but better than nothing. As 16-bit processors emerged, the IEEE defined a standard format for floating point that came to be accepted industry wide. This was IEEE-754-1985. It was revisited and updated in 2008. The chip manufacturers then developed hardware to implement the data structures and operations in the standard. Initially, these chips were coprocessors to the main (integer) ALU, but were included on the same chip as the technology advanced. Today, virtually all cpu's include a floating point unit.

Development of the IEEE standard

Standards help to keep everything consistent. We don't expect different answers from different brands of calculators. But back in the mainframe and minicomputer era, we got different answers based on the handling of floating point numbers differently by the various manufacturers. This is because a floating point value is not necessarily exact. It can be an approximation to the actual value. And, as calculations proceed, these same errors can add up. It was the same situation with the original implementations of floating point hardware chips. Different manufacturers handled situations such as rounding differently. Different answers resulted. That was to change in 1985, when the IEEE Standard for floating point was approved and adopted by industry. Before that, portability of programs between different brands of computers had to be carefully checked, and, in some cases, recoded.

In 1976, Intel was designing the floating point coprocessor for their x86 architecture. They were a key player in the early days of floating point, and their design would go on to heavily influence the standard. The standards effort spanned a decade, and had over 90 people involved directly.

One of the big issues that the standards committee tackled was the handling of underflow. This is the situation when a number gets close to zero, but is not actually zero. The number is not zero, but becomes smaller than the smallest representable number in the format. The standard does not guarantee a correct result. It does provide a level playing field of consistency and regularity.

The IEEE standard is revisited and modified as necessary about every ten to fifteen years. In 2008, a quad precision mode was added. Changes to the standard are handled very carefully, so as not to obsolete the millions upon millions of existing hardware units in use.

Software approaches

Floating point implementations on mainframes were unique to the manufacturer, DEC, IBM, and Univac each having their own design. DEC and IBM at least had several different designs. Converting between formats was a nightmare, and each package used different assumptions about round-off and overflow. As microprocessors emerged in the early 1970's the situation remained confused. Early processors could not support floating point directly.

Before floating point hardware, the operations would be carried out in software on the main cpu, a time-consuming operation. The software was referred to as the floating point library. It was a series of callable subroutines to implement the operations. Sometimes, this software was provided in a ROM.

Besides the four standard math functions, there was a need for calculation of trigonometric functions as well. This could be done rather easily in integer format, using the CORDIC algorithm. Cordic stands for coordinate rotation digital computer, and can be used even when the base hardware does not have a multiply instruction. It is still used in some basic embedded applications. It was originally developed in 1959 for the avionics computer of the B-58 aircraft, and generalized to handle exponentials, logarithms, multiplication, division, and square root. A decimal version was used in hand calculators. On cpu's, CORDIC usually uses a fixed point binary representation. A table of data stored in rom (or loaded in RAM) is used. CORDIC is an iterative process, but only uses add, subtract, and shift operations. CORDIC can be implemented in hardware, but requires the same complexity as a multiplier.

Motorola 6839 floating point rom

The 6839 chip provided floating point functions to Motorola's 6809 cpu. It was compatible with the IEEE Standard. It is not a coprocessor, but rather a set of floating point software routines in a ROM. The code was position independent (could be placed anywhere in the memory space). Operands could be placed in registers, or on the stack. Add's and subtracts took from 1200 to 3300 cycles, with multiply taking a maximum of 1600, and divide, about 3000. The clock speed of the 6809 processor was 2 MHz.

Floating point software package for the i8008 and 8080

A floating point software package was developed at the Lawrence Livermore Laboratory of the University of California for the Intel 8-bit 8008 and 8080 8-bit cpu's. This was done under contract to the U. S. Department of Energy in 1973. It was referred to in the project report as a "scientific notation mathematics package." The worst case timings for the operations were: add/subtract, 3 milliseconds; multiply, 7 milliseconds; divide, 8 milliseconds; and square root, 77 milliseconds.

The floating point format used a 24-bit mantissa, for 7 ½ digits of accuracy, and a 6-bit exponent. Thus, a floating point word took four 8-bit locations. The mantissa's were in sign-magnitude format, while the exponent was in 2's complement. The software checked for underflow and overflow. Input format conversion from BCD was provided, and an output routine would convert the result to printable ASCII format.

Numerous custom software packages for floating point calculations were developed, each using different formats. When floating point hardware started to emerge, the same situation occurred. However, the IEEE Standard for floating point rapidly became universally accepted, simplifying the whole situation.

The hardware

This section discusses the floating point coprocessors developed by the various chips manufacturers. Floating point operations were more complicated than fixed point, and the additional logic required a separate chips initially. As with the main cpu, early floating point units would occupy an entire circuit board of components.

Early in the develop of microprocessors, the dedicated calculator chips were more adept at advanced math than their integer counterparts. This was because the calculator chips could do calculations serially, because they only had to be as fast as the user could press keys. Calculators seem fast, but ask one to calculate a complex factorial, and watch them blink. Calculators used serial-by-digit calculation on BCD digits. Calculator chips found application as numeric coprocessors, such as the National Semiconductor MM57109. Modern day versions of these math coprocessors still exist, like the PAK series of co-processors from AWC Electronics for the simple STAMP micro-controller.

Before the IEEE standard for floating point was enacted, the formats for the numbers and the operations were defined by the manufacturer. This included the bit field sizes and the handling of rounding and overflow. The hardware at that time was generally called arithmetic processing units (APU), with the term floating point unit

(FPU) generally applied to units implementing the IEEE floating point standard.

Using the general term math coprocessor, these units handled the standard math operations (add, subtract, multiply, divide) on numbers in the floating point format. The earliest units only implemented Add, subtract, and multiply. Later units added transcendental functions such as trigonometric and log/exponential. These calculations usually implemented in microcode. The math coprocessors had their own registers to hold the two parts of the floating point numbers (signed mantissa, and signed exponent).

An integer cpu could generally view the math unit as a coprocessor that operated in parallel with the main cpu. Multiple coprocessors could be handled, subject to the architecture constraints of the main cpu. Generally, the main cpu fetched the floating point instruction, and passed it on to the coprocessor. The coprocessor could fetch its own data, using a dma-like protocol to request the use of the data bus from the main cpu.

The AMD 29C327 double precision floating point chip supported the IEEE Format, as well as DEC F (32-bit), D (32-bit), and G (64-bit) formats, and IBM System/370 double precision (64-bit) formats. It could also convert between supported formats. It implemented a 64-bit ALU and used 64-bit wide data paths. There were three input data ports, and a group of eight 64-bit registers. It supported 58 operations on floating point data, and could also convert floating point to integer. Comparison of floating point values was also supported. The instruction for the unit was 32-bits in length. Two of these chips could be used together in a master/checker mode. Here, the checker validated the results of the master's calculation, with the master unit comparing the results.

The Intel 8231 and equivalent AMD 9511 were arithmetic processing units, deployed before the IEEE standard was accepted. They were designed to interface with 8-bit processors; specifically, the i8080, and operated on 16 bit data. They implemented an 8-level stack. Operations were provided on 16-bit or 32-bit integer data, and 16- and 32-bit floating point. A sign-magnitude format for the mantissa and exponent were used. Operations included sin/cos/tan and their inverses; add, subtract, multiply and divide; e^x, y^x, and log base e; conversion between fixed and floating; The floating point value of pi was pre-programmed, and a floating point NOP was available.

The follow-on Intel 8232 and AMD 9512 were compatible with the IEEE-1985 standard. These units implemented a stack architecture, and communicated with the main cpu via a programmed I/O or DMA protocol.

41

For its 16 and 32 bit architectures, Intel developed a series of floating point coprocessors, the 8087, 80187, 80287, and 80387 that operated with their integer processors. There was no 80487, because Intel was able to implement that functionality on the same chip as the integer 80486 processor. The 80387 was the first Intel FPU to be fully compliant with the IEEE 754 standard. Previous units implemented a subset of the standard. AMD produced the FPU's in the Intel series under license, and went on to implement the functionality in their own line of IA-32-compatible chips (the 486, 586, K5, K6, K7, K8). Harris produced the x87 parts under license, as did Texas Instruments and ST.

The x87 architecture has an 8-deep data stack that holds items that can be directly accessed by offset from the top of the stack. Generally, a single operand will be at the top of the stack, and two operands will be at the top, and top plus 1. The x87 implements 32- and 64-bit integer arithmetic, and 80-bit IEEE floating point arithmetic. The units implement add, subtract, multiply, and divide, as well as square root, tangent, and arc-tangent.

The 80487SX chip was a strange device, designed to add floating point capability to the 486SX variant. The 386 and 486SX versions had 16-bit external data buses, but 32-bit internal data paths. They were intended to operate with less expensive memory. The i487SX was marketed as a floating point unit coprocessor for Intel i486SX machines. It actually contained a full-blown i486DX implementation. When installed into an i486SX system, the i487 disabled the main CPU and took over all CPU operations. The i487 took measures to detect the presence of an i486SX and would not function without the original CPU in place.

Cyrix developed its own x86 floating point coprocessor, the FastMath CX-83-D87, as part of the floating point wars. These chips were hardware compatible with the Intel main processors, but had additional functionality or increased speed. Cyrix integrated their FPU with their IA-32 architecture in the 6x86 chip.

IDT included floating point units in their C-series IA-32 chips. Chips &Technologies had their SuperMath series.

IIT produced compatible but faster FP chips, the 2C87 and 3C87. NexGen had their Nx587.

Weitek was a major floating point coprocessor vendor, with a line of Intel compatible, but not fully Intel floating point unit (x87) compatible units.

Weitek started out building general floating point processors. These were initially multi-chip architectures with separate adder (WTL1032) and multiplier (WTL1033) chips. They were sync-ed to the main ALU, and used 16-bit data buses. They implemented the IEEE single precision (32-bit) standard. The 1064/1065 models were 64-bit multiplier and adder. There are 32-bit wide ports for the device's. They handled IEEE single and double precision format, as well as DEC F (32-bit) and D (32-bit). They could convert between these formats and 32-bit integer.

Modern microelectronic circuitry has a complexity of hundreds of millions of switching transistors, and cannot be fully tested. This is because there are more possible states to test than the projected life of the universe would allow. Most of the time, many logic errors are never noticed. In one case, Intel's Pentium floating point unit has a bug in division (FDIV) that was not noticed for many years. It was discovered by a Professor at Lynchburg College in Virginia in 1994. An estimation at the time said the bug would result in inaccurate results in 1 case in 9 billion. The chips were recalled and replaced, after heavy pressure was brought to bear on Intel by the user community.

The 3C87 from IIT

This was another third-party IA-32 floating point coprocessor.

By the time of the Pentium IV, Intel and other x86 architecture manufacturers had integrated the floating point unit onto the same chips as the integer cpu.

Other Floating point chips

Floating Point coprocessor chips were not limited to the Intel X86 architecture. The Motorola 68881 and 68882 were floating point companion chips for the 68000 32-bit microprocessor. The chips implemented the IEEE standard. In this architecture, floating point instructions began with the hex digit F to make them easy to recognize in the instruction stream, and referred to as the "F-line" instructions. If a floating point processor were not present, an exception was generated, that could branch to a floating point software emulation routine. The 68881 had eight 80-bit data registers. It had seven different modes of numeric representation, including single-precision, double-precision, and extended-precision. The 68882 was an improved version of the chip, with a better pipeline, and capable of operating at higher clock speeds. It was pin-compatible with the older unit.

By the release of the advanced 68020 cpu, the interface with the floating point unit was simplified, with hardware support. The main cpu recognized FPU instructions, eliminating the need for the exception. By the release of the 68040 cpu, the floating point unit was integrated with the integer cpu.

Intel's i860, not an IA-32 architecture, had an integral floating point processor that was IEEE compliant. It could only divide by multiplying by the reciprocal, which it calculated by an iterative algorithm. Intel's i960 32-bit embedded processor did not have floating point capability.

The R3010 was the floating point chip for the MIPS R3000 series of processors. It featured a 6-stage pipeline, with separate calculation units for add/subtract, multiply, and divide, that operate concurrently. It was a follow-on to the previous R2010, for the R2000 cpu. These followed the IEEE 754 floating point standard. The 3010 finished operations in 1-19 clocks, using a 6-stage pipeline. It had 32 32-bit registers, that could be used as 16 64-bit registers, and was IEEE compatible. The R3010 featured bus snooping to recognize its instructions being fetched by the main cpu. This feature does not work with on-chip cache, that the FPU does not have access to.

In the advanced MIPS-II architecture, the chips were built from power-hungry but fast ECL technology. The R6010 Floating point controller was the adjunct unit for the R6000 cpu. There was also the choice of the B3110 floating point multiplier.

The National 32081 was the floating point chip for National's 32032 cpu. It was subservient to the main cpu, not a coprocessor. The cpu does the floating point unit's instruction and operand fetch. There was a 16-bit data bus between the two units. The fpu had eight 32-bit registers, which can be used in pairs as 64-bit registers. It was generally IEEE compatible.

For AMD's 29000 32-bit RISC chip, the 29027 was the floating point processor, a microprogrammed unit. The 29050 cpu had integral floating point capability, with a multiply-accumulate instruction for DSP-type operations, and a separate divide/square root unit. It also handled integer multiply.

Motorola's 88000 32-bit RISC chips was an integer processor, but the follow-on 88100 had integral floating point. There were separate add and multiply units. It achieved a performance around seven megaflops.

For HP's PA-RISC series, there were integral FP units, and also separate co-processors. These supported the new IEEE quad precision specification. There was also support for digital signal processing operations with multiply-accumulate and multiply-subtract instructions.

TDC1022/1042

These chips were 22-bit floating point units built by TRW Corp. They were, respectively, the adder and the multiplier. They implemented add, subtract, and multiply functions. The format was not IEEE compatible, with a 6-bit exponent and a 16-bit mantissa, both in 2's complement form.

The Zilog 8070

The Zilog 8070 arithmetic processing unit was designed to operate with Zilog's Z8000 32-bit cpu.

AMD 29325

The AMD 29325 implemented a 32-bit adder and multiplier processor. It supported IEEE single precision (32-bit) and DEC VAX F (32-bit) format. The associated 29323 chip was a 32-bit x 32-bit multiplier. These worked with the 29332 integer ALU. The 29325 also did integer to float, and float to integer conversion. It could also convert between IEEE (32-bit) and DEC format. Division was performed by multiplication by the reciprocal. The reciprocal was formed by a Newton-Raphson iterative process. This could be speeded up with a ROM-based table of the seed values for the iterative process.

Western Electric WE32106

The National 32000 32-bit cpu could use the Math Accelerator Unit (MAU) 32106 from Western Electric.

Analog Devices

Analog devices implemented the ADSP3210 32-bit x 32-bit floating point multiplier and ADSP322o floating point adder for digital signal processing applications. For multiplication, they use the Booth and Wallace tree algorithms. They are compatible with IEEE 32-bit format.

SPARC FP units

Numerous floating point units were available for the SPARC V8 and V9 architecture. These included the Weitek 1164/65, 8601, and 3170; the Texas Instruments 8847 and 602a; the Fujitsu 86903, and the Cypress 7C602. A version of the Cypress chips was developed for the European Space Agency's ERC32 SPARC-in-space chip set. Atmel's TSC692E is also a space-rated floating point processor for the ERC-32 chipset, implementing Space V8. It is fault tolerate and radiation hard.

B.I.T.

Bipolar Integrated Technology was an Oregon company making floating point units in Bipolar technology, a faster but more power hungry than the CMOS basis technology. The ECL versions were faster than the TTL implementation by a factor of five. Their B2120 floating point ALU chip was released in 1987. The associated multiplier chip was the B2110. These were TTL chips; later versions in ECL logic were the B3120 and B3110. The B4130 was an ECL combination of the ALU and multiplier in a single chip.

One of the first microprocessors to have an integral floating point unit was the Fairchild F9450, and implementation of the circa-1980 16-bit MIL-STD-1750A architecture. It implemented 32 and 48 bit floating point.

There are also general-purpose floating point units that are independent of their host's architecture. A current example of this is from Micromega, and consists of two chips that are essentially programmed Systems-on-Chips (SoC's) that implement floating point operations. The basic unit has essentially the same functionality as the first generation (8087-class) FPU's, such as fast 32-bit and 64-bit integer math, and IEEE format floating point. The larger unit adds features such as Fast Fourier Transform support, and GPS calculations. They have a large register set (128), and are low power and inexpensive. The 32-bit device is under $15.

And, in conclusion…

Floating point calculations are important. It is not exaggerating to say that the world depends on them for financial, engineering, and scientific calculations all the time. The timeliness of the results are fairly satisfactory, but we tend to view the accuracy and correctness as a given. Keep in mind, though, that floating point representation is an approximation, not a completely accurate result. In most cases, it is accurate enough. The handling of cases in which the accuracy could be impacted is defined by the standard, which had a lot of input from mathematicians. They didn't all agree on the handling of the rounding case, for example, where there are differing opinions. We have seen lives and expensive equipment lost due to floating point errors.

Perhaps it's best not to completely believe everything that comes out of a computer. Computers do make the mistakes we design into them.

Glossary

1's complement – a binary number representation scheme for negative values.

2's complement – another binary number representation scheme for negative values.

Accumulator – a register to hold numeric values during and after an operation.

ACM – Association for Computing Machinery; professional organization.

ALU – arithmetic logic unit.

ANSI – American National Standards Institute

APU – arithmetic processing unit

ASCII - American Standard Code for Information Interchange, a 7-bit code; developed for teleprinters.

ASIC – application specific integrated circuit.

Assembly language – low level programming language specific to a particular ISA.

Async – asynchronous; using different clocks.

BCD – binary coded decimal. 4-bit entity used to represent 10 different decimal digits; with 6 spare states.

Big-endian – data format with the most significant bit or byte at the lowest address, or transmitted first.

Binary – using base 2 arithmetic for number

representation.

BIST – built-in self test.

Bit – smallest unit of digital information; two states.

Blackbox – functional device with inputs and outputs, but no detail on the internal workings.

Boolean – a data type with two values; an operation on these data types; named after George Boole, mid-19th century inventor of Boolean algebra.

Borrow – mathematical operation when a digit become smaller than the limit and the deficiency is taken from the next digit to the left.

Buffer – a temporary holding location for data.

Bug – an error in a program or device.

Bus – data channel, communication pathway for data transfer.

Byte – ordered collection of 8 bits; values from 0-255

Cache – faster and smaller intermediate memory between the processor and main memory.

Carry – arithmetic result, when a digit is larger than a limit and the extra is moved to the left.

Chip – integrated circuit component.

Clock – periodic timing signal to control and synchronize operations.

Closely-coupled – two components operating together in a cooperative fashion.

CMOS – complementary metal oxide semiconductor; a technology using both positive and negative semiconductors to achieve low power operation.

Complement – in binary logic, the opposite state.

Control Flow – computer architecture involving directed flow through the program; data dependent paths are allowed.

Coprocessor – another processor to supplement the operations of the main processor. Used for floating point, video, etc. Usually relies on the main processor for instruction fetch; and control.

Cots – commercial, off-the-shelf.

CPU – central processing unit.

Digital – using discrete values for representation of states or numbers.

DMA - direct memory access (to/from memory, for I/O devices).

Double word – two words; if word = 8 bits, double word = 16-bits.

Dram – dynamic random access memory.

DSP – digital signal processor.

EIA – Electronics Industry Association.

Embedded system – a computer systems with limited human interfaces and performing specific tasks. Usually part of a   larger system.

Exception – interrupt due to internal events, such as overflow.

Fail-safe – a system designed to do no harm in the event of failure.

Fetch/execute cycle – basic operating cycle of a computer; fetch the instruction, execute the instruction.

Firmware – code contained in a non-volatile memory.

Fixed point – computer numeric format with a fixed number of   digits or bits, and a fixed radix point. Integers.

Flag – a binary indicator.

Flip-flop – a circuit with two stable states; ideal for binary.

Floating point – computer numeric format for real numbers; has significant digits and an exponent.

Flops – floating point operations per second.

FPGA – field programmable gate array.

FPU – floating point unit, an ALU for floating point numbers.

Full duplex – communication in both directions simultaneously.

Gate – a circuit to implement a logic function; can have multiple inputs, but a single output.

Giga - 10^9

Gigaflop – billion floating point operations per second.

Half-duplex – communications in two directions, but not simultaneously.

Handshake – co-ordination mechanism.

Harvard architecture – memory storage scheme with separate instructions and data.

Hexadecimal – base 16 number representation.

Hexadecimal point – radix point that separates integer from fractional values of hexadecimal numbers.

HP – Hewlett-Packard Company. Instrumentation and computers.

IEEE – Institute of Electrical and Electronic Engineers. Professional organization and standards body.

IEEE-754 – standard for floating point representation and operations.

Infinity - the largest number that can be represented in the number system.

Integer – the natural numbers, zero, and the negatives of the natural numbers.

Interrupt – an asynchronous event to signal a need for attention (example: the phone rings).

I/O – Input-output from the computer to external devices, or a user interface.

IP – intellectual property; also internet protocol.

IP core – IP describing a chip design that can be licensed to be used in an FPGA or ASIC.

ISA – instruction set architecture, the software description of the computer.

ISO – International Standards Organization.

ISR – interrupt service routine, a subroutine that handles a particular interrupt event.

Junction – in semiconductors, the boundary interface of the n-type and p-type material.

Kilo – a prefix for 10^3 or 2^{10}

Latency – time delay.

Little-endian – data format with the least significant bit or byte at the highest address, or transmitted last.

Logic operation – generally, negate, AND, OR, XOR, and their inverses.

LSB – least significant bit or byte.

Machine language – native code for a particular computer hardware.

Mainframe – a computer you can't lift.

Mantissa – significant digits (as opposed to the exponent) of a floating point value.

Master-helper – control process with one element in charge. Master status may be exchanged among elements.

Math operation – generally, add, subtract, multiply, divide.

Mega - 10^6 or 2^{20}

Megaflop – one million floating point operations per second.

Microcode – hardware level data structures to translate machine instructions into sequences of circuit level operations.

Microcontroller – microprocessor with included memory and/or I/O.

Microprocessor – a monolithic CPU on a chip.

Minicomputer – smaller than a mainframe, larger than a pc.

MIPS – millions of instructions per second; sometimes used as a measure of throughput.

MSB – most significant bit or byte.

Multiplex – combining signals on a communication c channel by sampling.

Mux - multiplex

NAN – not-a-number; invalid bit pattern.

NAND – negated (or inverse) AND function.

Negate – logical operation on data; changes the state.

Nibble – 4 bits, ½ byte.

NIST – National Institute of Standards and Technology (US), previously, National Bureau of Standards.

NOR – negated (or inverse) OR function

Normalized number – in the proper format for floating point representation.

Off-the-shelf – commercially available; not custom.

Opcode – part of a machine language instruction that specifies the operation to be performed.

OR – logical operation on data; output is true if either or both inputs are true.

Overflow - the result of an arithmetic operation exceeds the capacity of the destination.

Paradigm – a pattern or model

Paradigm shift – a change from one paradigm to another. Disruptive or evolutionary.

Parallel – multiple operations or communication proceeding simultaneously.

Parity – an error detecting mechanism involving an extra check bit in the word.

PC – personal computer, politically correct, program counter.

PCB – printed circuit board.

Pinout – mapping of signals to I/O pins of a device.

Quad word – four words. If word = 16-bits, quad word is 64 bits.

Queue – first in, first out data buffer structure; hardware of software.

Radix point – separates integer and fractional parts of a real number.

RAM – random access memory; any item can be access in the same time as any other.

Register – temporary storage location for a data item.

Reset – signal and process that returns the hardware to a known, defined state.

RISC – reduced instruction set computer.

ROM – read only memory

Semiconductor – material with electrical characteristics between conductors and insulators; basis of current technology processor and memory devices.

Semaphore –signaling element among processes.

Serial – bit by bit.

Shift – move one bit position to the left or right in a word.

SI – System Internationale; metric

Sign-magnitude – number representation with a specific sign bit.

Signed number – representation with a value and a numeric sign.

SOC – system on chip

Software – set of instructions and data to tell a computer what to do.

Stack – first in, last out data structure. Can be hardware or software.

Stack pointer – a reference pointer to the top of the stack.

State machine – model of sequential processes.

Synchronous – using the same clock to coordinate operations.

System – a collection of interacting elements and relationships with a specific behavior.

TRAP – exception or fault handling mechanism in a computer; an operating system component.

Truncate – discard. Cut off, make shorter.

TTL – transistor-transistor logic in digital integrated circuits. (1963)

Tri-state – logic device with 2 states, plus a high-impedance state

Underflow – the result of an arithmetic operation is smaller than the smallest representable number.

Unsigned number – a number without a numeric sign.

Vector – single dimensional array of values.

VHDL- very high level description language; a language to describe integrated circuits and asic/ fpga's.

Via – vertical conducting pathway through an insulating layer in a semiconductor.

Von Neumann, John, a computer pioneer and mathematician; realized that computer instructions are data.

Wiki – the Hawaiian word for "quick." Refers to a collaborative content website.

Word – a collection of bits of any size; does not have to be a power of two.

XOR – exclusive OR; either but not both.

Selected Bibliography

AMD, *32 bit Microprogrammable Products, Am29C300/29300 Data Book*, 1988.

AMD, *Am29325 32-bit Floating Point Processor*, Nov. 1984.

ANSI/IEEE Standard 754-1985 for Binary Floating-Point Arithmetic, IEEE Computer, Jan. 1980.

Barrenechea, Mark J.; "Numeric Exception Handling", Programmer's Journal, May 1991, v9 n3 p 40.

A. Bartoloni, C. Battista, S. Cabasino, N. Cabibbo, F. Del Prete, F. Marzano, P.S. Paolucci, R. Sarno, G. Salina, G.M. Todesco, M. Torelli, R. Tripiccione, W. Tross, P. Vicini and E. Zanetti, *MAD, A FLOATING —POINT UNIT FOR MASSIVELY—PARALLEL PROCESSORS,* 1991, CERN,
https://s3.cern.ch/inspire-prod-files-f/fc7223a232785fb9b3ab2a1867d38ddc

Beebe, Nelson H. F. *New Directions in Floating-Point Arithmetic*, AIP Conference Proceedings. 12/26/2007, Vol. 963 Issue 2, p 155-158.

Birman, M.; Samuels, A.; Chu, G.; Chuk, T.; Hu, L.; McLeod, J.; Barnes, J. "Developing the WTL3170/3171

"Sparc floating-point coprocessors," Micro, IEEE, Feb. 1990, Vol. 10, Issue 1, pp 55 – 64.

Cavavagh, Joseph *Digital Computer Arithmetic Design and Implementation*, 1984, McGraw Hill, ISBN 0-07-010282-1.

Coone, Jerome T. "An Implementation Guide to a Proposed Standard for Floating-Point Arithmetic," IEEE Computer, January 1980.

Erle, M.A. Hickmann, B.J.; Schulte, M.J. *Decimal Floating-Point Multiplication* . IEEE Transactions on Computers, July 2009, Vol. 58, Issue 7, pp.: 902 – 916.

Fandrianto, Jan and Woo, B. Y. "VLSI Floating-Point Processors," 1985, IEEE CH2146-9/85/000.

Goldberg, David *What Every Computer Scientist Should Know About Floating-Point Arithmetic*, March, 1991, Computing Surveys, 1991, Association for Computing Machinery.

Hwang, Kai *Computer Arithmetic, Principles, Architecture, and Design*, Wiley, 1979, ISBN-0471034967.

Intel, *80387 Programmer's Reference Manual*, 1987, Intel, 231917-001.

Koren, Israel; Zinaty, Ofra "Evaluating Elementary Functions in a Numerical Coprocessor Based on Rational Approximations," IEEE T. Computers, Vol. 39, No. 8, August 1990, pp. 1030-1037.

Kuki, H.; Cody, W. J. *A Statistical Study of the Accuracy of Floating Point Number Systems,* Communications of the ACM (CACM), Volume 16 Issue 4, April 1973, Pages 223 – 230.

Kulisch, Ulrich W.; Miranker, Willard L. *Computer Arithmetic in Theory and Practice*, Academic Press, 1981. ISBN- 012428650X.

Maples, Michael D. "Floating Point Package for Intel 8008 and 8080 Microprocessors," Oct. 24, 1975, Lawrence Livermore Lab, University of California.

Maurer, P.M. "Design verification of the WE 32106 math accelerator unit," Design & Test of Computers, IEEE, June 1988, Vol. 5 , Issue 3, pp. 11 – 21.

Minagi, Yukinari Kanasugi, Akinori "A Processor with Dynamically Reconfigurable Circuit for Floating-Point Arithmetic," World Academy of Science, Engineering & Technology. Aug 2010, Vol. 68, pp. 1128-1132.

Motorola, MC68881/882 *Floating Point Coprocessor User's Manual*, 1989, 2nd ed., Prentice-Hall, ISBN 0-13-567009-8.

Motorola, *DSP96002 IEEE Floating-Point Dual Port Processor User's Manual*, Motorola, DSP96002um/ad, 1989.

Muller, Jean-Michel; Brisebarre, Nicolas; de Dinechin, Florent; Jeannerod, Claude-Pierre; *Handbook of Floating-Point Arithmetic,* Birkhäuser; 2010 edition, ISBN-081764704X.

Overton. Michael L. *Numerical Computing with IEEE Floating Point Arithmetic*, Society for Industrial & Applied Math; 1st edition, 2001, ISBN-0898714826.

Parker, Richard O. *Am29027 Handbook*, AMD, 1989, ASIN B000734M5Y.

Rowen, Johnson, and Ries "The MIPS R3010 Floating Point Coprocessor", IEEE Micro, June 1988.

Scott, Norman R. *Computer Number Systems & Arithmetic*, 1985, Prentice-Hall, ISBN-0-13-164211-1.

Sharma, Shubhash Kumar, Srivastava, Vishal Kumar, Jha, Udai Kumar *Development of Radix-Independent Floating-Point Arithmetic for IEEE 854 Standard,* International Transactions in Applied Sciences; Jul, 2011, Vol. 3 Issue 3, p387-396.

SPARC Architecture Manual, Version 8 Appendix N, "SPARC IEEE 754 Implementation Recomendations."

SPARC Architecture Manual, Version 9, Appendix B, "IEEE Std. 754-1985 Requirements for SPARC-V9."

Sterbenz, Pat H. *Floating-Point Computation,* Prentice Hall; 1st ed, 1974, ISBN-0133224953.

Stakem, Patrick H. *A Practitioner's Guide to RISC Microprocessor Architecture,* Wiley-Interscience; 1st edition, 1996, ISBN-0471130184.

Tambascia, Nicola *Introduction to numeric precision and representation issues: why 4.8 minus 4.6 is not always equal to 0.2*, Pharmaceutical Programming. Dec 2011, Vol. 4 Issue 1/2, p107-113.

Winkler, Jürgen F. H. *Konrad Zuse and Floating-Point Numbers*, Communications of the ACM; Oct 2012, Vol. 55 Issue 10, p6-7, 2p.

Resources

www.cpu-world.com

http://grouper.ieee.org/groups/754/

http://micromegacorp.com

wikipedia, various.

If you enjoyed this book, you might also be interested in some of these.

Stakem, Patrick H. *16-bit Microprocessors, History and Architecture*, 2013 PRRB Publishing, ISBN-1520210922.

Stakem, Patrick H. *4- and 8-bit Microprocessors, Architecture and History*, 2013, PRRB Publishing, ISBN-152021572X,

Stakem, Patrick H. *Apollo's Computers,* 2014, PRRB Publishing, ISBN-1520215800.

Stakem, Patrick H. *The Architecture and Applications of the ARM Microprocessors,* 2013, PRRB Publishing, ISBN-1520215843.

Stakem, Patrick H. *Earth Rovers: for Exploration and Environmental Monitoring,* 2014, PRRB Publishing, ISBN-152021586X.

Stakem, Patrick H. *Embedded Computer Systems, Volume 1, Introduction and Architecture*, 2013, PRRB Publishing, ISBN-1520215959.

Stakem, Patrick H. *The History of Spacecraft Computers from the V-2 to the Space Station*, 2013, PRRB Publishing, ISBN-1520216181.

Stakem, Patrick H. *Floating Point Computation*, 2013, PRRB Publishing, ISBN-152021619X.

Stakem, Patrick H. *Architecture of Massively Parallel Microprocessor Systems*, 2011, PRRB Publishing, ISBN-1520250061.

Stakem, Patrick H. *Multicore Computer Architecture,* 2014, PRRB Publishing, ISBN-1520241372.

Stakem, Patrick H. *Personal Robots*, 2014, PRRB Publishing, ISBN-1520216254.

Stakem, Patrick H. *RISC Microprocessors, History and Overview,* 2013, PRRB Publishing, ISBN-1520216289.

Stakem, Patrick H. *Robots and Telerobots in Space Applications*, 2011, PRRB Publishing, ISBN-1520210361.

Stakem, Patrick H. *The Saturn Rocket and the Pegasus Missions, 1965,* 2013, PRRB Publishing, ISBN-1520209916.

Stakem, Patrick H. *Visiting the NASA Centers, and Locations of Historic Rockets & Spacecraft,* 2017, PRRB Publishing, ISBN-1549651205.

Stakem, Patrick H. *Microprocessors in Space*, 2011, PRRB Publishing, ISBN-1520216343.

Stakem, Patrick H. *Computer Virtualization and the Cloud*, 2013, PRRB Publishing, ISBN-152021636X.

Stakem, Patrick H. *What's the Worst That Could Happen? Bad Assumptions, Ignorance, Failures and Screw-ups in Engineering Projects, 2014,* PRRB Publishing, ISBN-1520207166.

Stakem, Patrick H. *Computer Architecture & Programming of the Intel x86 Family, 2013,* PRRB Publishing, ISBN-1520263724.

Stakem, Patrick H. *The Hardware and Software Architecture of the Transputer*, 2011,PRRB Publishing, ISBN-152020681X.

Stakem, Patrick H. *Mainframes, Computing on Big Iron*, 2015, PRRB Publishing, ISBN- 1520216459.

Stakem, Patrick H. *Spacecraft Control Centers*, 2015, PRRB Publishing, ISBN-1520200617.

Stakem, Patrick H. *Embedded in Space,* 2015, PRRB Publishing, ISBN-1520215916.

Stakem, Patrick H. *A Practitioner's Guide to RISC Microprocessor Architecture*, Wiley-Interscience, 1996, ISBN-0471130184.

Stakem, Patrick H. *Cubesat Engineering*, PRRB Publishing, 2017, ISBN-1520754019.

Stakem, Patrick H. *Cubesat Operations*, PRRB Publishing, 2017, ISBN-152076717X.

Stakem, Patrick H. *Interplanetary Cubesats*, PRRB Publishing, 2017, ISBN-1520766173 .

Stakem, Patrick H. Cubesat Constellations, Clusters, and Swarms, Stakem, PRRB Publishing, 2017, ISBN-1520767544.

Stakem, Patrick H. *Graphics Processing Units, an overview*, 2017, PRRB Publishing, ISBN-1520879695.

Stakem, Patrick H. *Intel Embedded and the Arduino-101, 2017,* PRRB Publishing, ISBN-1520879296.

Stakem, Patrick H. *Orbital Debris, the problem and the mitigation*, 2018, PRRB Publishing, ISBN-*1980466483.*

Stakem, Patrick H. *Manufacturing in Space*, 2018, PRRB Publishing, ISBN-1977076041.

Stakem, Patrick H. *NASA's Ships and Planes*, 2018, PRRB Publishing, ISBN-1977076823.

Stakem, Patrick H. *Space Tourism*, 2018, PRRB Publishing, ISBN-1977073506.

Stakem, Patrick H. *STEM – Data Storage and Communications*, 2018, PRRB Publishing, ISBN-1977073115.

Stakem, Patrick H. *In-Space Robotic Repair and Servicing*, 2018, PRRB Publishing, ISBN-1980478236.

Stakem, Patrick H. *Introducing Weather in the pre-K to 12 Curricula, A Resource Guide for Educators*, 2017, PRRB Publishing, ISBN-1980638241.

Stakem, Patrick H. *Introducing Astronomy in the pre-K to 12 Curricula, A Resource Guide for Educators*, 2017, PRRB Publishing, ISBN-198104065X.

Also available in a Brazilian Portuguese edition, ISBN-1983106127.

Stakem, Patrick H. *Deep Space Gateways, the Moon and Beyond*, 2017, PRRB Publishing, ISBN-1973465701.

Stakem, Patrick H. *Exploration of the Gas Giants, Space Missions to Jupiter, Saturn, Uranus, and Neptune*, PRRB Publishing, 2018, ISBN-9781717814500.

Stakem, Patrick H. *Crewed Spacecraft*, 2017, PRRB Publishing, ISBN-1549992406.

Stakem, Patrick H. *Rocketplanes to Space*, 2017, PRRB Publishing, ISBN-1549992589.

Stakem, Patrick H. *Crewed Space Stations,* 2017, PRRB Publishing, ISBN-1549992228.

Stakem, Patrick H. *Enviro-bots for STEM: Using Robotics in the pre-K to 12 Curricula, A Resource Guide for Educators,* 2017, PRRB Publishing, ISBN-1549656619.

Stakem, Patrick H. *STEM-Sat, Using Cubesats in the pre-K to 12 Curricula, A Resource Guide for Educators,* 2017, ISBN-1549656376.

Stakem, Patrick H. *Lunar Orbital Platform-Gateway,* 2018, PRRB Publishing, ISBN-1980498628.

Stakem, Patrick H. *Embedded GPU's,* 2018, PRRB Publishing, ISBN- 1980476497.

Stakem, Patrick H. *Mobile Cloud Robotics,* 2018, PRRB Publishing, ISBN- 1980488088.

Stakem, Patrick H. *Extreme Environment Embedded Systems,* 2017, PRRB Publishing, ISBN-1520215967.

Stakem, Patrick H. *What's the Worst, Volume-2,* 2018, ISBN-1981005579.

Stakem, Patrick H., *Spaceports,* 2018, ISBN-1981022287.

Stakem, Patrick H., *Space Launch Vehicles*, 2018, ISBN-1983071773.

Stakem, Patrick H. *Mars*, 2018, ISBN-1983116902.

Stakem, Patrick H. *X-86, 40th Anniversary ed*, 2018, ISBN-1983189405.

Stakem, Patrick H. *Lunar Orbital Platform-Gateway*, 2018, PRRB Publishing, ISBN-1980498628.

Stakem, Patrick H. *Space Weather*, 2018, ISBN-1723904023.

Stakem, Patrick H. *STEM-Engineering Process*, 2017, ISBN-1983196517.

Stakem, Patrick H. *Space Telescopes,* 2018, PRRB Publishing, ISBN-1728728568.

Stakem, Patrick H. *Exoplanets*, 2018, PRRB Publishing, ISBN-9781731385055.

Stakem, Patrick H. *Planetary Defense*, 2018, PRRB Publishing, ISBN-9781731001207.

Patrick H. Stakem *Exploration of the Asteroid Belt*, 2018, PRRB Publishing, ISBN-1731049846.

Patrick H. Stakem *Terraforming*, 2018, PRRB Publishing, ISBN-1790308100.

Patrick H. Stakem, *Martian Railroad,* 2019, PRRB Publishing, ISBN-1794488243.

Patrick H. Stakem, *Exoplanets,* 2019, PRRB Publishing, ISBN-1731385056.

Patrick H. Stakem, *Exploiting the Moon,* 2019, PRRB Publishing, ISBN-1091057850.

Patrick H. Stakem, *RISC-V, an Open Source Solution for Space Flight Computers,* 2019, PRRB Publishing, ISBN-1796434388.

Patrick H. Stakem, *Arm in Space*, 2019, PRRB Publishing, ISBN-9781099789137.

Patrick H. Stakem, *Extraterrestrial Life*, 2019, PRRB Publishing, ISBN-978-1072072188.

Patrick H. Stakem, *Space Command*, 2019, PRRB Publishing, ISBN-978-1693005398.

CubeRovers, A Synergy of Technologys, 2020, PRRB Publishing, ISBN-979-8651773138.

Robotic Exploration of the Icy moons of the Gas Giants. 2020, PRRB Publishing, ISBN- 979-8621431006

Hacking Cubesats, 2020, PRRB Publishing, ISBN-979-8623458964.

History & Future of Cubesats, PRRB Publishing, ISBN-979-8649179386.

Hacking Cubesats, Cybersecurity in Space, 2020, PRRB Publishing, ISBN-979-8623458964.

Powerships, Powerbarges, Floating Wind Farms: electricity when and where you need it, 2021, PRRB Publishing, ISBN-979-8716199477.

Hospital Ships, Trains, and Aircraft, 2020, PRRB Publishing, ISBN-979-8642944349.

<u>2020/2021 Releases</u>

CubeRovers, a Synergy of Technologys, 2020, ISBN-979-8651773138

Exploration of Lunar & Martian Lava Tubes by Cube-X, ISBN-979-8621435325.

Robotic Exploration of the Icy moons of the Gas Giants, ISBN- 979-8621431006.

History & Future of Cubesats, ISBN-978-1986536356.

Robotic Exploration of the Icy Moons of the Ice Giants, by Swarms of Cubesats, ISBN-979-8621431006.

Swarm Robotics, ISBN-979-8534505948.

Introduction to Electric Power Systems, ISBN-979-8519208727.

Centros de Control: Operaciones en Satélites del Estándar CubeSat (Spanish Edition), 2021, ISBN-979-8510113068.

Exploration of Venus, 2022, ISBN-979-8484416110.

Patrick H. Stakem, *The Search for Extraterrestial Life,* 2019, PRRB Publishing, ISBN-1072072181.

The Artemis Missions, Return to the Moon, and on to Mars, 2021, ISBN-979-8490532361.

James Webb Space Telescope. A New Era in Astronomy, 2021, ISBN-979-8773857969.

www.ingramcontent.com/pod-product-compliance
Lightning Source LLC
La Vergne TN
LVHW092345060326
832902LV00008B/819